exploring shapes

An Aladdin Book
© Aladdin Books Ltd 1998
Produced by
Aladdin Books Ltd
28 Percy Street
London W1P OLD

First published in Great Britain
in 1998 by
Aladdin Books/Watts Books
96 Leonard Street
London EC2A 4RH

ISBN 0-7496-3174-0

Project Editor: Sally Hewitt

Editor: Liz White

Design

David West • CHILDREN'S BOOK DESIGN

Designer: Simon Morse

Photography: Roger Vlitos

Illustrator: Tony Kenyon

Printed in Belgium

The author, Andrew King, is an experienced teacher.
He currently works for the London Borough of Richmond
as an advisory teacher for mathematics. He works with
children and runs courses for teachers.

The project editor, Sally Hewitt, is
an experienced teacher. She
writes and edits books for children on a
wide variety of subjects including science,
music and maths.

MATHS *for fun*

exploring
shapes

Andrew King

Aladdin / Watts
London • Sydney

CONTENTS

INTRODUCTION

You can see interesting shapes everywhere. Architects use shapes to build houses, bridges and machines. Artists make amazing patterns with shapes. You can make beautiful tessellating patterns and fascinating puzzles and games when you learn about two- and three-dimensional shapes.

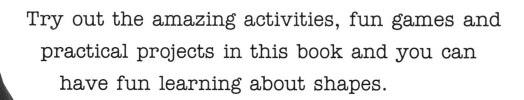

Try out the amazing activities, fun games and practical projects in this book and you can have fun learning about shapes.

● Follow the STEP-BY-STEP INSTRUCTIONS to help you with the activities.

● Use the HELPFUL HINTS for clues about the experiments and games.

● Look at FURTHER IDEAS for information about other projects.

1 Yellow squares mean this is an easy activity.

2 Blue squares mean this is a medium level activity.

3 Pink squares mean this is a more difficult activity. You'll have to think hard!

SQUARES AND RECTANGLES

What do you know about squares? They have four corners and four sides, but do you know what is special about them? The sides are all the same length and the angles at the corners are all the same. Rectangles' corners are all the same angle and their opposite sides are the same length.

THE BLACKHOLE

1 Two players must try to cover a piece of paper with rectangles, without falling down the black hole! You need paper, coloured pencils and a ruler.

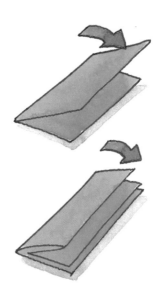

2 To make the grid for the game fold a piece of paper in half lengthways as shown in the picture. Repeat this three more times. Unfold the paper and do the same, folding from top to bottom.

3 Unfold the paper and draw lines along the folds to make your grid. Choose any square and draw the blackhole.

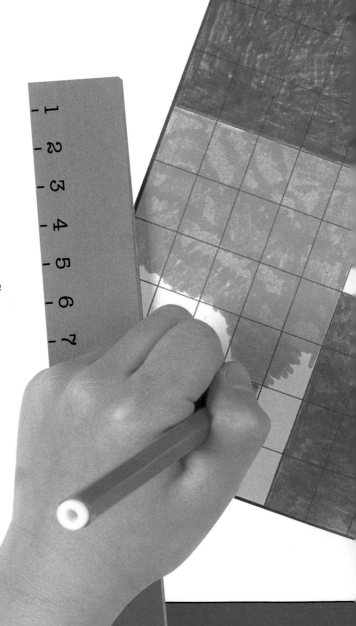

4 Players take turns to colour in a rectangle following the lines of the grid. You could draw a rectangle that takes up lots of spaces or one that takes up just one space if you like. Avoid the black hole, if you draw over the blackhole you lose!

HELPFUL HINTS

● A ruler might help you to draw the sides of the rectangle straight.

● You can draw a square on the grid because a square is a rectangle too!

FURTHER IDEAS

● If you are good at playing The Blackhole try Sea Monsters!

● Make the grid again but this time draw four sea monsters on it.

● Can you draw in rectangles that avoid the hungry beasts?!

TESSELLATIONS

Do you have any tiles in your house? There might be some in the kitchen or bathroom, on the walls or on the floor. The tiles are often square shaped because they fit together easily, leaving no gaps. When a shape fits together like this we say the shape **tessellates**.

TESSELLATING TILES

You can use squares to make interesting tessellating shapes. You will need some paper, thick card, a compass, tape, scissors, a pencil and coloured pens.

1 Cut out a square of card with sides of about 5cm.

2 Cut out a part of the square and move the part to the opposite side of the square like this.

3 Join it to the other side of the square with some sticky tape. Place your new tile in the middle of the paper and draw round it lightly with a pencil.

4 Pick up the tile and place it so it fits in with the first outline. There shouldn't be any gaps! Keep repeating this across the page until it is covered.

5 Outline the tiles with a thick pen and decorate the tiles with a bright pattern.

HELPFUL HINTS

● You can make a square with a compass. Open the arms about 5cm apart. Place the point at the corner of the page (A) and make a mark with the compass along the two edges of the paper (B and C). Place the compass point on B and mark an arc, do the same on C. Where the arcs cross mark D. Use the ruler to join A, B, C and D and cut out your square.

FURTHER IDEAS

● Try making more complex tile patterns by cutting out more than one part of the square.

● Make sure you move the part you have cut to line up exactly on the opposite side of the square.

THE THIRD DIMENSION

Shapes that are flat, like squares and rectangles have two **dimensions**, length and width. Three-dimensional shapes like cereal packets and cans also have height. Some box packets can be undone and flattened. When this is done you can see the two-dimensional shapes, called faces, it is made from. The flat unfolded shape is the **net** of the box.

FISHING NETS

Find a die. How many faces does it have? What shape are they? There are six square faces. We call this shape a cube. If you could unfold the cube to make a net what would it look like?

1 Make six equal squares from card, these will be the six faces of the cube. Draw a fishing net and fish on each of the faces.

2 Arrange the squares with one or more of their sides together to make a net for a cube. If your net were folded, would it make a cube?

3 Tape the squares on the plain sides and try folding the net into a cube. Does it work? If it does, unfold it again and draw a picture of the arrangement of the squares.

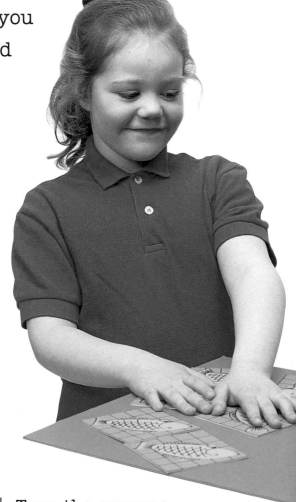

4 Can you find another way of arranging the squares into a net that makes a cube?

5 There are lots of different nets that make a cube. How many can you find?

TRIANGLES

I'm sure you know what a triangle is but did you know how amazing they are!? You can use them to make many shapes with any number of straight sides. Take these triangles for a 'walk' and see what shapes you can make!

WALKING TRIANGLES

1 Draw out any triangle with a ruler on a piece of card. Cut it out carefully. Mark one of the corners with a pen on the front and back.

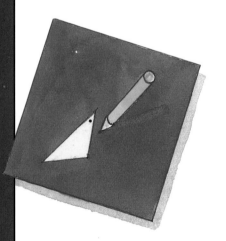

2 Put your triangle on a piece of paper. The marked corner stays fixed, it does not ever move from that spot. Draw round the triangle.

3 Now, flip over the triangle keeping the marked point fixed and the edge of the outline touching the card like this. Draw round the triangle again.

4 Keep repeating this until the triangles you have drawn are about to overlap. Draw round the edge of your shape with a ruler and colour in the triangles carefully and make some beautiful patterns.

HELPFUL HINTS

● When you draw round your triangle do it lightly and quickly with a pencil. If you make a mistake it is easy to rub it out later. Remember you will be going over the lines later with pens and a straight ruler.

FURTHER IDEAS

● Don't stop drawing the triangles when they are about to overlap.

Keep walking the triangle! What happens to the shape that you make? Go on, get carried away!

MORE TRIANGLES

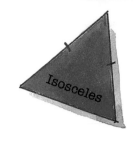

Did you know there are different types of triangles?

An isosceles triangle has two sides of equal length - the marks show which sides are equal.

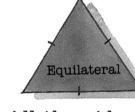

All the sides of an equilateral triangle are the same length.

A right-angled triangle has one corner that looks like the corner of a square.

A scalene triangle has no equal sides.

TROTTO!

1 Trotto can be played by two, three or four players. To play, make 12 cards. On each card draw a triangle, make sure you draw 3 of each type. Draw in the marks on the equilateral, isosceles and right-angled triangles.

2 Find a die and cover each face with blank stickers. Write 'miss turn' twice, 'scalene', 'isosceles', 'equilateral', 'right-angled' on the faces.

3 Deal out the cards. Place them on the floor face up. Take it in turns to throw the die. If it shows one of your triangles turn it over and pass the die to the next player.

4 The winner is the first player to turn over all their cards!

HELPFUL HINTS

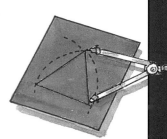

● Equilateral triangle: Draw a line and open the compass to the length of the line. Put the compass point on one end of the line and draw an arc. Put the point on the other end of the line and draw another arc. Draw a line from where the two arcs cross to each end of the line.

● Isosceles triangle: Draw a short line. Open the compass so it is longer than the line. Draw two arcs as you did above. Draw a line from where the arcs cross to each end of the line.

● Right-angled: Make a right angle measurer by folding any sized scrap of card roughly in half. Fold it again so the folded edge meets itself neatly. Draw along the straight edges of your measurer then join the ends of the line with a ruler.

● Scalene: Easy! Just draw a triangle with no equal sides.

PYRAMIDS

A tetrahedron might sound like an alien from outer space, but it's not! It is a three-dimensional shape, a pyramid with four faces. What makes a tetrahedron special is that all four faces are triangles. It is also called a triangular-based pyramid. You have probably seen other pyramid shapes, like those in Egypt. Square-based pyramids have four triangular faces and one square face.

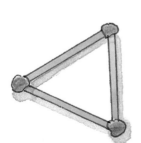

PYRAMID SKELETONS! Dare you attempt the pyramid skeleton challenge!?

1 If you feel brave enough you will need some straws, scissors and plasticine.

2 Cut six straws to about 10cm long.

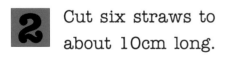

3 Join three straws in a triangle with the plasticine.

4 Now stick a straw in each of the three corners and bend them over until they meet at the top. Secure them with some more plasticine.

● You don't need to measure each straw with a ruler to get the same length. A quick way of doing it is to cut one to the length you want then use that straw as a measure against the other straws.

5 You have made the skeleton of a tetrahedron. Can you make a skeleton of a square-based pyramid with eight straws?

FURTHER IDEAS

● Try making a star skeleton. You will need 36 straws of the same length. Don't make the straws too long otherwise the skeleton might become weak. Make a cube from 12 of the straws.

● On each of the faces make a pyramid with four more straws. In no time at all you will have made a beautiful star!

CIRCLES

Trace round a plate on some paper and cut it out. You can find the centre of the **circle** by folding it in half twice. The centre is where the folds meet. Draw a line along the fold that crosses the centre of a circle. This line is called the **diameter**. The length of the circle's edge is called the **circumference**.

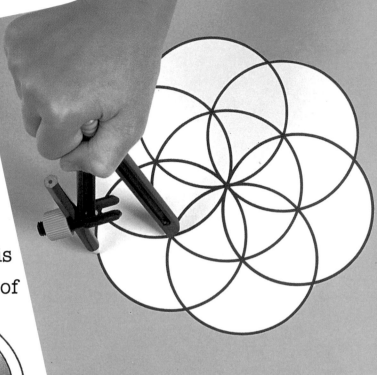

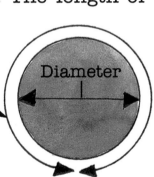

Diameter

DRAWING DAISIES

1 You can make beautiful flower shapes drawing circles! All you need is a compass, paper, pens and pencils.

2 Draw a circle in the middle of a piece of paper. Pick up the compass but don't move the arms! Place the point anywhere on the circumference and draw another circle.

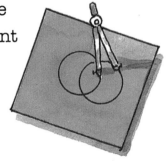

3 Put the point of the compass on one of the places where the two circles meet and draw the third circle.

4 Draw a fourth circle where the edge of two of the circles meet like this. Keep drawing circles until you have made a lovely pattern.

5 Now you can decorate your flower with beautiful colours and make a fabulous display!

HELPFUL HINTS

● You don't have to have a compass to make these patterns. It is easy to make your own circle drawer!

● You will need a piece of card, scissors, a drawing pin and a pencil. Cut out a strip of card. Make a hole with the pin at each end of the card. Leave the pin in the card and push the pencil through the other hole. Now you can draw lots of circles!

FURTHER IDEAS

● Try drawing different patterns. First draw a circle then place the point of the compass on the edge and draw another circle. Draw a third circle where the two meet. Now mark all the points on the edge of the shape where two circles meet and draw three more circles. Repeat this as many times as you like. Do you notice a tessellating pattern?

STRETCHING CIRCLES

Shapes can be changed by making them bigger, smaller and in many other ways too. One interesting way of changing circles is to stretch them. When a circle is stretched it becomes oval or an ellipse.

PULLING FACES

1 To pull faces you need more than your own face and a mirror! Find an old photograph or a picture of a face from a magazine. Make sure the face fills as much of the picture as possible.

2 Place a compass point at the centre of the face and lightly draw as large a circle as possible. Cut out the circle.

3 Turn it upside down and cut lines across the circle from one side of the face to the other about six or seven times like this. You could make your cuts straight or wiggly.

4 Turn the strips face up and put them back into a circle. Now stretch them out leaving the same space between each piece and make a funny face! Stick your funny face onto card.

HELPFUL HINTS

● Pictures from magazines are often on thin paper. Make your picture stronger by sticking some card to the back. Now draw the circle and cut it out.

FURTHER IDEAS

● Try stretching other shapes like a square or a triangle or your own made-up special shapes.

● You could try a different type of stretch like this one below.

CENTRES, SECTORS AND CONES

When you draw a circle with a compass, the compass point is the centre of the circle. The distance between the centre and the edge of a circle is called the **radius**. If you draw a line from the centre to the edge of the circle it will always be the same length. If two lines are drawn it looks as though a wedge of cake has been cut. This wedge is called a sector.

Radius

HATS

It is great fun designing party hats! To make your hats you will need plenty of coloured card, pens, scissors, sticky tape, a compass, streamers and sticky shapes to decorate your hats.

Sector

1 Draw a large circle on some card with your compass. Now draw the radius. Draw another radius. You could make the sector either wide or narrow.

2 Cut out the circle and the sector and carefully stick the edges of the larger sector together like this. You have now made a **cone**!

HELPFUL HINTS

● To help the hats stay on your friends' heads make a small hole on the inside of the hat on each side close to the ears. Thread some elastic through the hole. Tie a knot, to stop the elastic slipping back through the hole and do the same on the other side.

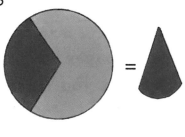

3 Last of all decorate your hat with sticky shapes and streamers!

FURTHER IDEAS

● Experiment by cutting out different sizes of sectors from the circles.

How does it change the shape of the cone?

● Cutting out a large sector will make the hat more pointed. If you cut out a small sector the hat will stay quite flat.

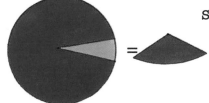

POLYGONS

A **polygon** is a flat two-dimensional shape with three or more straight sides. Some have special names. A pentagon has five sides, hexagons have six sides. Heptagons have seven sides. Octagons have eight sides.

FEELY SHAPES

If you don't know the names of shapes, how well can you describe them?

1 Three or more players can play Feely Shapes. You will need some card, scissors, pencils, a ruler, paper and a bag to hide the shapes you make.

2 Draw some shapes on the card. The lines must be straight but can be any length and the corners can be any angle.

Now cut them out and put them in the bag.

3 One of the players chooses a shape inside the bag. They must keep it hidden and describe it to the other players without looking at it!

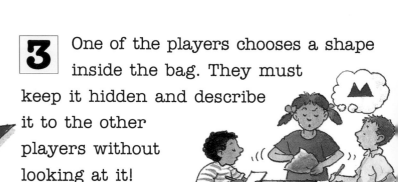

4 The other players try and draw the shape that is being described. When the other players have finished their sketches, take the shape out of the bag.

HELPFUL HINTS

● With some practice you can become very good at describing polygons.

● Try to describe the number of straight sides. Do they feel long or short?

● What do the corners of the shape feel like? Are they very pointed?

FURTHER IDEAS

● Try playing the same game again but this time include shapes with curved edges, like circles and ellipses or your own made up shape!

5 The winner is the player that has made the best drawing of the polygon.

TANGRAMS

A tangram is an ancient Chinese shape puzzle a little bit like a jigsaw. Some people think tangrams are about 2,500 years old! It is made up of five triangles, a square and a parallelogram which is another four-sided shape.

CATS AND DRAGONS

To make the tangram shapes you need a square of thin card, pens, ruler, and a pair of scissors.

1 Draw a grid of 16 squares on the card like this. Copy the tangram shapes from below with a pen and ruler.

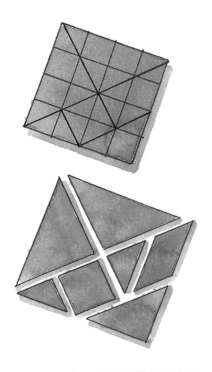

2 Cut out the seven shapes from the card. Mix them up on the table. Can you put them back together again to make a square? Challenge your friends, too, and see if they can make a square!

3 Perhaps you found that easy! But can you arrange all seven shapes to make a rectangle?

4 Try making a cat shape with the tangram pieces. Remember you must use all seven pieces.

HELPFUL HINTS

● You can make the grid for the tangram by folding the square piece of thin card in half. Fold it in half again in the same direction. Unfold the square and repeat the folding from top to bottom. Your card is now ready for you to copy the tangram shapes.

FURTHER IDEAS

● Why not make up your own tangram puzzle? Each puzzle must use all seven pieces.

● First arrange your pieces carefully on some paper. Draw round the outline lightly in pencil.

● Go over the outline again using a ruler and a pen to make it clearer. Last of all, give your puzzle a name like 'the dragon' and challenge a friend to match the tangram shapes to your puzzle.

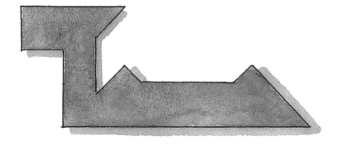

POLYHEDRA

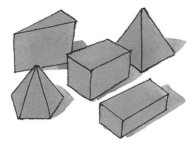

A **polyhedron** is a three-dimensional shape. It can have any number of faces. A tetrahedron has four triangular faces and a cube has six square faces. How many faces do you think an octahedron has? That's right, eight faces!

BUILD IT!

If you look carefully around your home you can find lots of different shapes: a packet of cereal, a cylinder from the inside of a toilet roll, a ball, a die or cube. Perhaps you have some toy building bricks.

1 To play Build It! you need two of each shape. Collect about five pairs of identical shapes. If you want to you could paint them all the same colour, but check with an adult first.

2 Now sit back to back with a friend. Build a model with all your shapes but make sure your friend can't see!

3 Try to describe how your model is built as clearly as you can. Can your friend match your model exactly?

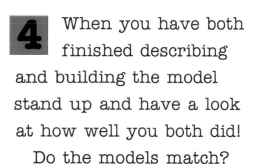

4 When you have both finished describing and building the model stand up and have a look at how well you both did! Do the models match?

HELPFUL HINTS

● It helps to describe the position of each shape. You might say...

the cube is on top of
or
to the right of
or
underneath
or
next to
or
touching the corner of

How else can you help your partner?

FURTHER IDEAS

● Collect some more three-dimensional shapes and play this fun memory game.
Put all the shapes on a table and let your friends have a good look. Now your friends turn away and you remove one of the shapes. Change round the position of the remaining shapes then shout 'ready!' Your friends now have to try and guess which shape you have taken!

COMMON SHAPES

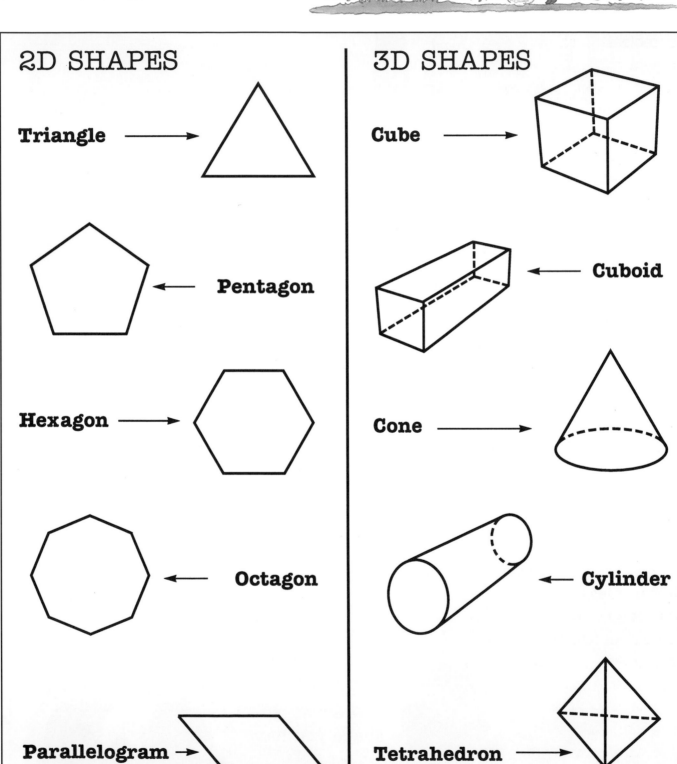

2D SHAPES

Triangle →

Pentagon ←

Hexagon →

Octagon ←

Parallelogram →

3D SHAPES

Cube →

← **Cuboid**

Cone →

← **Cylinder**

Tetrahedron →

GLOSSARY

Circle

A circle is a round shape with one curved edge. The distance from the centre of the circle to any point on its edge is always exactly the same.

Circumference

The circumference is the length all the way round the edge of a circle.

Cone

A cone is a solid shape. The base it stands on is a circle. Its curved surface goes up to a point at the top.

Diameter

The diameter is a line that cuts a circle exactly in half. It goes from the edge of the circle, through the centre and to the edge on the other side.

Dimension

We use dimensions to measure shapes. Flat shapes like circles or squares are 2D because they have two dimensions. We can measure how long and how wide they are. Solid shapes like cones and cubes are 3D because they have three dimensions. We can measure how long, how wide and how high they are.

Net

A net is a flat shape made when the sides of a solid shape, like a cube, are opened out. When the net is folded and the sides are joined together it makes a solid shape again.

Polygon

A polygon is any flat shape that has three or more straight sides. A square, a triangle and a rectangle are all polygons.

Polyhedron

A polyhedron is any solid shape that has four or more flat sides called faces. A cube is a polyhedron with six faces. An octahedron is a polyhedron with eight faces.

Radius

The radius is the distance from the centre to the edge of a circle. Any straight line drawn from the centre to the edge of a circle is called a radial line.

Tessellation

A tessellation is made when lots of flat shapes are fitted together in a repeating pattern with no gaps between them.

INDEX